Breaking Free:

Living Beyond the Lies that Our Mothers Taught Us!

Charlotte M. Watson

Castanitta

Blessings to you

as you Live life on

+ m Purpose!!

Your Sista

Charlotte M. Watson

ISBN: 09985482656
ISBN-13: 9780985482657

DEDICATION

To my mom and best friend,
I have been taught many lessons watching you walk through
life's difficult days with strength, grace and a head held high.
Thank you for showing me how to accept Christ
as the lover of my soul!
I could never repay you for all the sacrifices
that you made for our family!

Linda Ruth Derrough-Walker, my aunt and the only sister I knew.
You were my confidant, adviser and friend.
Many of these conversations took place
years ago as we talked through some of life's situations.
I can't wait to see you again and catch up!

To my Daddy, Billy Frank Watson and my grandfather,
W.H. Derrough, I have been amazingly blessed to
have been loved by men like you.
I love you both all the way to heaven!

CONTENTS

ACKNOWLEDGMENTS

Like the turtle on the fence post, I am indebted to those who have helped me get to this point. These dear friends and family members have labored with me and sacrificed for me, allowing me to give birth to this message. I offer special thanks and gratitude to:

To my brothers- Phillip, Frederick, Patrick and yes, you too, Charles! Life is worth living because you love me. Thank you for being who you are. I love you to the moon and back.

To my best friend, who is surely dancing in the heavenly streets and choreographing the steps. Your love for Christ was so infectious! Thank you for your friendship, your teachings and for putting your theological eyes on the pages, before leaving us so soon! You are missed tremendously.

Finally, all of heaven will know how grateful I am to you, Lord Jesus, when I get to you. It is by your word that I have been set free. Thank you, Father. I love you!

FOREWORD

Rarely have I read a book with which I so deeply identify. I found myself filled with hope and at the same time broken and ashamed at the way that we have allowed the world to dictate how Christians Woman/Marriage should be. For the last fourteen years I've not only been an advocate for healthy relationships, and marriages. But holding woman accountable and allowing them to understand their role and responsibilities as a wife. I love how Charlotte Watson stated that this book be used as a "toolkit, and practical wisdom." I could not agree with her more stating that we need to break free from the lies, that has been passed down from generation to generation regarding relationships. Especially the chapter that talks about "What Happens in this House Stays in this House". This has ruined so many relationship, and kept us in such bondage. Because *Therefore there is now no condemnation for those who are in Christ Jesus. Romans 8:1 NASB.* This Scriptures and all the scriptures listed will help us free ourselves from bondage. This is a very good reference, and will allow us to memorize those verses that will help us to break free from those lies, stories and even experiences that we held on to while we were growing up.

I am really a big fan on self-care! IF you know me, you know I have to get my hair done every week. Charlotte breaks it down with Jesus, Others, and Yourself = JOY. IF you don't take care of yourself then you are no good for anyone else. How can you be accountable to someone else when you are not able to take care of yourself. We are not SUPERWOMAN that is why you have a help-mate that God has given to you. Then the Lord God said, it is not good for the man to be alone; I shall make him a helper suitable for him" Gen 2:18. If we only see what is right there and use the help that we have. It will use to incorporate the tips that Charlotte gave us for taking better care of ourselves. If we begin to incorporate these tools into our daily lives, then we would be able to take care of our husbands!

Submission is such a touchy subject when it comes to relationships, and women. We see submission as being beneath, are behind. Submission is side, by side. Charlotte could not have said it any better "Submission is easy when it's reciprocated of a husband's leadership". The faster we understand our role as a wife, this makes the transition to becoming a wife so much smoother.

Charlotte's book, *Breaking Free: Living Beyond the Lies that Our Mother's Taught Us*, is a real gift to all woman, she has certainly hit two of the four obstacles that hit couples within their marriage. That is Finance, and Intimacy. If there was a topic in the mists of misunderstanding and miscommunication, it is woman perception are idea of marriage. *Breaking Free: Living Beyond the Lies that Our Mother's Taught Us* allows us to break free from the bondage, of what we thought marriage looks like. It has given a clear and better understanding of what God design for marriage should be. So ladies "let's break free, lean on each other, hold each other accountable and continue to walk in the new truth that has set you free!"

Lavida Davison,
Licensed Professional Counselor

Breaking Free: Living Beyond the Lies that Our Mothers Taught Us

Introduction

Growing up, we can remember things that were taught to us. Then there were other things that were "caught" by us. No one ever really said it, but we saw it and duplicated it. However, we gained this helpful and hurtful knowledge. This learned lessons have since shaped our lives, our relationships and the lenses that we view things from. These lessons have shaped our decisions in raising our children, how we interact in our gender based relationships and even how we interact with other cultures and ethnicities . As the popular artist, Kirk Franklin sings, the truth can hurt us or heal us. That is the reason for this work that was impressed upon me to share with each of you.

For some, you will have to push past the fear, the hurt, the bitterness and the pain to allow the healing to begin. From a medical perspective, if a patient pulls out the IV because it hurts, they will never get to see the benefit of the medicine at work. So, as you begin to read through these passages, I am going to ask you to commit to pushing past every hindrance that the enemy will bring to light and place in your way, physically or emotionally. So that we don't give the enemy too much credit, know that the enemy often is the one staring back in the mirror at us. We can be our biggest hindrance.

For others, you are in a place of spiritual maturity. Your situations have caused you to redirect some things in your life and you have created a lit pathway for others to follow and trot right on in to victory. I am going to ask that you commit to being that spiritual midwife. Each one of us has a purpose that God so wants fulfilled. If you are walking in yours, let's reach out and help someone gain the strength that they need to walk into theirs.

Whoever you are, I pray that you take a moment to reflect on how we can move to a place of victorious living. I am charging each of us today, to take our misery and use it for ministry. Turn our pain into positive power and take our words of wisdom to help strengthen others on this journey called life!

I am praying for you and walking this journey with you! Keep in touch. I want to hear the stories of God's transformative power that He will work in your lives.

Now, my sister, let the breaking begin!

Your sister,

Charlotte

CHAPTER 1
ARE YOU MY MOTHER?

Mother- 1a. A female parent; 1b. A woman in authority spiritually; 2a. The superior in a religious community or women; 2b. An old or elderly woman.

Although this is the technical online definition, we would all agree that mothers come in different forms and the word mother is used in different ways. From what I can tell, there are 6 types of mothers. Even in its wide use, it is most commonly defined as one who gives birth. But depending on your culture, background or environment, it could be one's older sister who has taken on the role of mother. We can't forget the church mother, who will surely pull you to the side and lovingly instruct you that it's time to be introduced to a panty girdle or slip. Don't know what a panty girdle is? Today, we call them spanks. It's a thicker panty that supports the backside from any shaking, jiggling or movement that may cause inappropriate looking from the young boys sitting on the back row. And heaven forbid, that one outspoken church mother who repeatedly tells the girls to keep their purses closed and tells the boys to keep your pencils in your pockets if you know what I mean. Many ladies have step mothers. I simply like to refer to them as the mother of a blended family. Then there's the godmother, who vows to step up if the mother is absent for any reason. Finally, we have an older female or aunt that you looked up to as a mother. So, whatever package your mother came in, girls have all learned countless lessons in a variety of ways from these mothers.

Now before I go any further, let's look at that word learned. Keep in mind that to learn something or to acquire information or a skill, it doesn't necessarily require someone to formally go through a lesson presentation. I am sure you have heard the saying, and I quote, "Do what I say, not what I do." Well, many times girls find themselves picking up what has been said and what has been seen. What am I trying to say? I am glad you asked! Some of those learned lessons are spoken, but just as many are unspoken, seen behaviors. Some of these lessons are positive and some are negative, but all learned and passed down from mother to mother; no doubt, by these influencers who have taken on the role of mother. Some of these lessons were witnessed in action; how they interacted with their husbands, their sons or other men in their lives. Furthermore, we can see these lessons as they maneuvered through the inner personal relationships and the countless number of conversations that transpired day in and day out with mothers, family members, and church friends. Perhaps we heard the "after church" conversations over the phone with "Sister Sally". Perhaps it was the "Aunt Mae" who you could always expect to see helping herself to another plate at Sunday dinner or the annual family reunion. Maybe it was none of those at all. Per chance, you were a witness to someone you love become a victim of domestic violence and you vowed to never let it happen to your child. The nights you cried yourself to sleep, pleading with God to make the fighting stop! Whether good or challenging experiences, our lives are shaped and molded by these occurrences that we have been afforded firsthand knowledge of. So, from our mothers, we pass beautiful and sometimes bitter lessons on to our daughters, nieces and other young ladies. Every lady is a student of these lessons while we are on this journey called life.

Rest assured that this project is not a means to condemn our mothers for what they didn't know. Your mother and mine did the very best that they could with the information that they had. Yet, it's a book that is the result of hours of research, with friends, ministers, counselors, business women and "domestic engineers". It is a result of self-reflection and countless conversations with women; some young, some seasoned, various nationalities, a myriad of ethnicities and different faiths...all sharing one common thread...experiences that shaped their lives and one common effect.... hurts and pains. These pains have shaped and directed their lives into many directions and many different pathways. Many of our decisions in life are direct or indirect results of these incidences that have occurred in our lives.

This book is designed for your active participation. As you take some time to explore this journey to freedom, I'd like for you to find a sister who you can be accountable to. Consider walking this process out with someone you can trust; another sister who has achieved victory. Sisterhood, per the urban dictionary, says that sisterhood is a bond between two or more girls, not always related by blood. They always tell the truth, honor each other, and love each other like sisters.

Now that definition is just the kind of sisterhood I'm talking about and that every girl needs! Telling each other the truth, in love, of course, honoring each other (building up not tearing down) and loving each other like sisters (to uphold you when you are right and talk you out of the wrong)! What prevents us from having that kind of sisterhood? I would like to submit to you today that our experiences have caused heart blockages (things that have hurt our hearts that we can't get passed). Our fears of having open-heart surgery (intentionally dealing with those issues) have allowed them to cause toxins (bitterness, bad attitude, un-forgiveness, etc.) to enter into our bodies. Many of our blockages have permeated such toxins throughout our hearts and minds that we are unable to truly love, value and honor ourselves, so we obviously can't reciprocate that to others. Unfortunately, we have seen how to live with a mask on as we suffer in silence within the four walls of our homes. What's in the past stays there, we are told! So, day in and day out we live a life that is built on lies, all the while in fear that someone will see the real us. How about the woman fashioned by the designer clothes, on point with hair, makeup and eyelashes. She's living in the beautiful brick house with the white picket fence, driving the expensive family car, sporting the doting husband, mothering the 2.5 kids, walking the dog inside the gated community and all the "stuff" in between. We see this diva and immediately put her down, engage in the conversations of she thinks she's all that and become envious and jealous hearted. Truth be told, many of these sisters are empty, lonely and crying on the inside. Come on sister, it's time for a Holy Ghost shake down! It's time to break free!

My prayer is that this short book, used in the form of a toolkit, will provide nuggets of practical wisdom. We can take these biblical principles to build our strength, to break free from these very lies that are responsible for unhealthy relationships. These relationships start with us, but permeate to others from our past, present, and the future to come. These are lessons that have been learned along the way and have continued to keep us in a holding pattern that limits our fulfillment. I am referring to thoughts that have been influenced by our sisters, aunts, mothers, cousins, coworkers, and friends and yes, maybe even some enemies. All of these personal relationships throughout our lives thus far have created the lessons in the areas of money, relationships, and sexual intimacy. The challenge is to truly and honestly, look at the woman in the mirror. Be honest about the pain that has happened to you, whether self-inflicted or induced by someone else. **Reflect** on what and who the woman in the mirror has become. **Repent** for adopting and holding on to the non-productive behaviors that we were "taught". **Rejoice** for the sound wisdom that we have received placing us where we are today and what will propel us into our Christ filled purpose. Then lastly, **Regroup**. Now, this is the tricky part. Regrouping means we must be willing to openly receive and apply these practical nuggets, even if it requires us to break some things off and out of our lives. The things we must break off if we want to be free and victorious, are the behaviors that we have justified for years. Speaking of nonproductive behaviors, we have to hold ourselves accountable for gossiping, jealousy and tearing down others. Whether we know them or not our attitudes, our hurtful words and sharp tongued comments and having the need to have the first and the last word has become a part of what we do. This regrouping may even mean that we must shake off people who are in our lives that we know are toxic. As you are reflecting, be honest with yourself and allow your sister to be honest with you. The things that have hindered our yesterday and could potentially hinder our future are the very things that must be addressed. Now be prepared, some of these unproductive behaviors will not be favorable and likely not be societal and culturally popular. Oh sure, the world applauds us and our social media friends may continue to "like" and "react" to our posts, but our Father is not pleased, nor moved by behaviors that hurt his heart. Breaking free of these things not only benefit us individually, but we can then flourish into being better mentors to the next generation while being true and consistent examples of our faith. It's important that we are examples to our families and to a world of young women who need Godly examples of healthy females demonstrating how to manage and maintain their relationships. This example first begins with the relationship that you have with God and yourself. Although this journey will focus on five lies, my hope is that this will open you up to explore other myths or lies that we have allowed to become our badge of honor. Through examining these life mottos that have not always produced the best fruit in your life, it will spark a revolution of reigniting a lost sisterhood where we can stand and proudly say to each other:

I respect you enough to receive God's truth in love.
I trust you enough to share my inner pains, hurts, and struggles.
I love you enough to allow you to examine with me my destructive
and unhealthy behaviors, so that I have an accountability partner.
Because We Are Our Sister's Keeper!
So, take a deep breath, take your sister by the hand and let's start this
journey together, today, right now! Let's shake these lies off so that
we can Break Free and truly live the life that our Father has for us!

CHAPTER 2
WHAT HAPPENS IN THIS HOUSE STAYS IN THIS HOUSE!

Cynthia Daniels, a nine-year-old running around on a hot Texas summer day. While playing outside with her friends, "Cynthia, I am out of sugar," her mother calls. "I need you to go down the street to Sister Parks' and ask her for 2 cups of sugar. I'm making the last pound cake for the church picnic." Now everybody knows that Sister Daniels makes the best buttermilk and sour cream pound cake in town. So when the church picnic comes around, the pastor calls on you know who to make enough pound cake to go around. "Yes, ma'am", Cynthia responds as she skips out hurriedly for those 2 cups of sugar. "Hurry back, now. I'll call her and let her know you are on your way." Cynthia arrives at Sister Parks' and rings the doorbell. Deacon Parks, Sister Parks husband and well respected deacon at the church, answers the door and invites her inside. She tells him that she's there to get the sugar that her mother called about. "Well, she is not here. She went down to the church and I am not sure how long she will be gone", Deacon Parks. explained. "But I can get the sugar for you." "Thanks", replied Cynthia as he leads her into the kitchen. Just as Deacon Parks was about to present the container of sugar, he turned and said, "Now it's going to cost you." Cost me what, she thought. Momma didn't send me with no money! As she reached for the container of sugar, the man that she had grown to know as a father figure and a leader in her church says, "Give Ol' Dec a hug and some of yo' good ole' sugar too." He reaches out to hug Cynthia, but this time he didn't let go. This hug was different thnt the hug that he gave at church, It just didn't feel right. "Now don't you make a sound, you hear. Ole Deac just want to show you how special you are." As he held her body close to his, he began to rub her shoulders. She felt his hands move slowly down her back. Tears began to stream down her face. "It's ok baby. Deac' not gonna hurt you. You are too special for that." Soon his had skid down her thigh, then slowly between her legs. This can't be right, she thought to herself. "Momma and Daddy told me I can't let nobody touch me there," she said in a strong but soft voice, as tears now gushing from her eyes. "Awh, they know how special you are, so there aint no need in you telling them about me. Besides, they ain't gonna believe you, no way. You just another little fass girl running around the neighborhood," he said convincingly. Just as Ole Deacon Parks began to unzip his pants, the sugar jar that was sent for went crashing to the floor. That was her chance to get out of there. Cynthia pushed away and headed as fast as she could out of that house. With a fountain of tears streaming from her cheeks, this scared and confused little girl said to herself, "They will too believe me; You just wait and see. I'm going to tell my daddy!"

Mothers hear their names called in many different ways and situations. But there is a particular high screeching sound when a mother's name is called when she knows that there is something wrong. As Cynthia burst into the house calling for her mother, her mother knew something was wrong with her child. As Cynthia recounted every detail of her encounter with Ole Dec, tears began to roll down her mother's face. She took Cynthia in her arms and hugged her as tight as ever. "I am so sorry child. It will be alright," Momma consoled. "I'll talk to your daddy when he gets home and we will get this all straighten out. Now go to your room and lay down 'til dinner is ready. Cynthia," Mom called as she turned to walk away. "Don't go telling nobody about this, you hear. This is our business. What happens in this house, stays in the house. Do you understand?" a reluctant "Yes, Ma'm" was returned by Cynthia.

Not long after, Cynthia heard voices in the kitchen. Dad was furious, but Mom, in her soft and gentle voice convinced Daddy to let

Pastor King handle it. Pastor King, promised to confront Deacon Parks inappropriate and sinful behavior. He promised Daddy that he was sure that he would address the situation and it would never happen again.

Church was awkward for Cynthia, especially the greeting period. Although Cynthia's mother and father made sure to sit away from Deacon Parks so that hugging wouldn't take place, it still felt uncomfortable. But no matter how strange it felt, nothing was ever said of that dreadful day again.

This is a story all too familiar. Different details and different names, but the result is the same. When and if the "Cynthias" of the world muster up enough courage to tell that influential female, did she look the other way or at worse, blame her for being "fass". Although it may never be discussed or brought up again, it is certainly far from forgotten. You put it in the back of your mind, close the mental door to the emotional room and throw away the key. How many of you know that just because you don't think about it, doesn't mean that it disappears? Hello? Do you hear me now? Not only does it resurface from time to time, but it brings some well-known partners with it...guilt, shame, un-forgiveness, and maybe even anger that grows into bitterness if never addressed.

What happens in this house stays in this house, is not what we consider an unspoken rule at all. This rule was not only spoken, but it was often imprinted and sometimes reinforced with a braided switch (two or three small branches braided together), cowhide belt or if really needing to make an impression, a razor strap. This lie was one that was imprinted into our minds (by way of our backsides) by a many a mother. Every...not ten, not fifty, but every woman that I questioned about this saying was familiar with this rule. From as early as each one could remember, their mothers gave this family oath in her strong voice of "and don't let me have to tell you again" voice. I am certain that in that mother's heart, she felt that she was doing the right thing to make sure her family laundry didn't become the local breaking news at the corner five and dime, local beauty shop or Lawd help us, at the annual church picnic!

Although I have heard my grandmother include in hundreds of conversations, "The road to hell is paved with good intentions," I am certain that my mother, your mother, our mothers, all had good intentions. This infamous one liner lesson of secrecy is behind thousands, upon thousands of undisclosed hurts and debilitating pains that have been silenced in the hearts of young and seasoned "Cynthias" alike. During our discussions, these conversations quickly moved from a simple question to ministering to women who began, after all these years, to uncover centuries of abuse by uncles, fathers, step-fathers, brothers, and mother's boyfriend and yes, even husbands. The scriptures have much to say about secrets. But Luke 8:17 is the one that speaks to me the loudest. The Amplified Bible says it like this,

> For there is nothing hidden that will not become evident, nor anything secret that will not be known and come out into the open.

Now before you just start saying Amen and breaking out in to a shout of praise, listen and allow the words to penetrate. The word 'nothing' is in the same category as the word 'all'. Dr. Sony Ocho says, "there is nothing on the other side of all. So All means All." I am saying, there is nothing on the other side of nothing! So nothing means absolutely... nothing. If nothing is hidden that will not be evident, that means THERE IS **NOTHING** HIDDEN that **WILL NOT** be made evident. Got it, good!! Now you can start that shout of praise! So, you see, it doesn't matter if we keep it in the house. If it happened in secret, told all of our lives to keep it a secret, you may as well up the covert secret agent uniform and badge, because it will eventually be uncovered. End of story! Grandma used to say, "what's done in the dark will come to light." Now, HOW and WHEN it will be known and come out into the open, well that is the question that only you can let us in on. Several ways that the enemy will attack us is through guilt, fear and shame. If he can cause emotional damage to your inner being, shame and guilt will quickly set in. Now if he can paralyze you with fear from sharing, a seed of self-worthlessness begins to grow and you will become a prisoner to negative outlooks on life and relationships, even with the way you treat yourself. Sometimes it's so subtle that we don't even recognize that we are carrying a seed of un-forgiveness and anger that turns into bitterness and negativity. Wait, hold on...but I am a Christian and I go to

church!! Don't shoot the messenger, but that's all we are doing... just professing and just going to our places of worship. I know, I know, you serve in the

God uses every experience in your past as a building block for your future!

hospitality ministry, in the choir, dressed in our first lady suits and hats and maybe even in the pulpit. But unfortunately, we are no better than we were ten, twenty and fifty years ago! Our growth is stunted and we are failing to produce any kind of fruit that will benefit humanity. Emotionally, we are still in that childhood state of feeling shameful, angry and hurt, so we lash out and continue unhealthy, un-Christ-like behaviors as a result of it. When will we stop this age old emotional rollercoaster and get off? Well my sister today is a mighty good day to hit the emergency stop button! The sooner you make the decision to break free from this lie, the sooner you can be healed. Although *God uses every experience in your past as a building block for your future*, you have a responsibility. If you are serious about stopping the pain and letting go of the bitterness, it starts by you making the decision to not be held hostage another day! Sister, today is your day to break free and live!

So, let's go to a scripture. Come on now; read it for yourself so you don't think this is my own ingenious point. Although there are various verses about abuse, let's just look at a few and commit to making them apart of our emotional escape route. Read with me Psalms 103:6. It says,

> The Lord give righteousness and justice to all those who are
> treated unfairly.

Oh my! Does that not just make you want to high-five God! This is sound proof that our God is sovereign over our past and our today! No matter what has happened, he has us completely covered and defended our honor. He can and will not only address our perpetrator, but he can address them better than we could ever plan to. So why are we continuing to hold to those issues that are still causing us pain?

You should be shouting for joy right now! I mean, I am writing it and can hardly contain myself. That is some good news ya'll! And if that isn't enough, let's park in Isaiah 43:18-19. The Message version of the bible makes it as clear as Belizean ocean water. It says:

> Forget about what's happened; don't keep going over old history.
> Be alert, be present, I'm about to do something brand-new.

OMG!! (That means **O**h **M**y **G**oodness, for all of you non-texters). Somebody hold my pen!.....Do you see what this means? Whatever has happened to us, has happened. It's sad, frustrating, hurtful and painful. But we can't go back and change it. What we can do is trust God to care for our future. He promises that if we cry out to him when we are in trouble, that he will save us from our distress. Psalms 107:20 says through his word we are healed. But you have to be willing to receive it, believe it and walk in it. Notice I didn't say talk it and tell it. God is more concerned about our walk than he is about our talk.

Not only do we feel pain from our past, but many times the guilt and shame of those incidents will not let us forget. Just when we think that we are past thinking about what happened, the enemy will craft up something in our hearts and minds. In his craftiness, he strategically convinces us that we are responsible for things that we had no control or power over. Ladies, that is a lie from the pit of hell that should be returned to its sender. The word tells us in Hebrews 10:22 that:

Let us go into the presence of God with true (sincere) hearts, fully trusting him. For our guilty (evil) consciences have been sprinkled with Christ's blood to make us clean, and our bodies have been washed with pure water.

So nothing that the enemy says to you can over-ruled or contradict what Christ has told you in his word. God will not only heal the pain, but he will heal the guilt and the shame that we carry around from day to day. Don't you see how one little seemingly harmless statement, "What Happens in this House Stays in this House", can affect us in such a powerful way that it keeps us in bondage? It's just one seed that bears fruit to so many ungodly actions in our lives.

Well now, let's wrap this up. If Christ is going to give righteousness and justice for being treated unfairly, remove guilt and shame that we are deceived with, what in the world is left for you to feel and hold on to? I mean...you just read it... IT'S ALL GONE!! IT'S ALL GONE!! IT'S ALL GONE!!   Thank you, Jesus! It is all gone! We don't have to hold on to it anymore.

Closing Thoughts - Reading scripture is good, but what do we do tomorrow, next week or next month when we must, literally, remember our past or look our abusers in the face? Taking one day at a time, allow God to give us just what we need for each day...Let's take the plunge together and start right now, praying that the power that God has already given us will be activated in order to break free from the guilt, the shame and the un-forgiveness that has plagued us. Just remember, **God uses every experience in our past as building blocks for our future!** But for now, my sister, let's celebrate! No More Guilt...No More Shame... No More Shackles...No More Chains...It Is Over... It Is Finished... You are on your way to be Free!

*Reflections*_____

_____

_____

_____

_____

_____

Prayer to Break Free

Thank you, Father for your loving kindness and your unfailing love that you have shown me. I recognize and declare that there is no other name that can save, deliver and restore me. I need you, Lord, to show me how to forgive, starting with my own forgiveness. Deliver me from the behaviors that have kept me from trusting your word. Help me to forget those things that are behind, so that I can move in to what you have ahead for me. You alone are my redeemer. I am trusting that you will remove the enemy imposed guilt that I have lived with for so long. I pray that those who have wronged me will come to your knowledge and turn their heart to you. I declare today that I am shaking off the lies that I have learned and adopted as a way of life! I am committing today to be transparent and sincere to you first God, so that I may be healed. I love you Lord, for you are my strength and my redeemer.

Amen

CHAPTER 3
HOME IS YOUR <u>FIRST</u> PRIORITY

The alarm sounds at 5:00 a.m., hours before the sound of little feet hit the floor and shortly before the sound of gargling in the shower. Hours before cars are heard moving about the often-busy street, from around the corner she comes, barely out of bed and on a mission down the hall with what seems to be…. a laundry basket of clothes in her arms? Yes, that's exactly what it is! But wait, it appears that she is stopping in the kitchen to start a pot of coffee. Now moving to the laundry room and starting the washer for that load of clothes that was sorted the night before. Time to get dressed for work, wake the kids for school, get hair combed, teeth brushed, clothes on, breakfast on the table, lunches made, a quick routine kiss to the spouse and now the race to work is on! And that's all before 7:00 a.m.

The work of a mother is never done with the many hats she wears. And wouldn't you know it; the evening schedule is none the less jammed packed as the first part of the day. She's off to chauffer the kids who have their own people to see and places to go. They are picked up from school, rushed in for a snack and headed off to, well let's just take your pick: tutoring, football, volleyball, soccer, dance, music lessons, karate, PTA, open house, praise team, church choir rehearsal and the list goes on and on. Then what's waiting for mom's return is dinner, dishes, laundry to go into the dryer and yes, homework too! Finally, the kids are ready for baths and soon after that, hallelujah…its bedtime! So, she gladly tucks everyone in, with prayers being the welcomed benediction for the night. She puts the dishes away, secures the doors and puts the last stack of folded clothes away. Finally, she drags her exhausted body into bed for the night. Just as a sigh of relief escapes her tired and worn body, a tap on the shoulder and a twinkle in his eye is the recipe for a "sho'nuf" catfight! Lord, you have got to be kidding me!

Although somewhat a little humorous, how many of you have seen this episode play out in your own lives? We have been told that "Home is Priority", so we have learned to wear the Super Mom and Wife title as a badge of honor! I would like to submit, that home **is** **not our first** priority. Right after Christ, WE are priority! I can hear the voice of my grandmother, Fannie B. Derrough, "When you have ten children, a husband and have to go to the field, you don't have time to think about yourself." Now, don't get me wrong, there is absolutely nothing wrong with striving to be the best wife and mother that you can be. Most of us didn't realize that when we got the titles of wife and mother, we also received a few others as bonuses: mediator, counselor, chauffer, teacher, tutor, chef, doctor, nurse, referee, laundress, seamstress, baker, dishwasher, sweeper, household maid, nurturer, protector, encourager, beautician, friend, just to name a few. How in THE world can anyone do and be all of that every single day, every week, every month, every year for the rest of their lives? Well... by NOT making your home priority. Hold your horses! I promise I will explain it so that it makes sense.

Maybe your story goes a little differently. Maybe you are a single parent and there's no one to help you get the kids ready for school, to drop them off or even pick them up. It's all on you, mom. So you do the best you can at juggling all the pieces. Heaven knows one little hiccup and everything will come crashing down. Home...priority? Even in a 2 parent household there is a percentage who feels that they can hardly get anything done. Between work, midweek service, if we can squeeze it in, kid's soccer, dance and a husband who "Lord, Have Mercy" becomes the battle cry! Listen lady, God doesn't need your Plan of Action. What he is looking for is your Faith put into

Action! What I am trying to say is, that you are responsible for making yourself a priority. If we say that he is the lover of our souls, we have to be willing to give him time that he needs to love on you and replenish you each day.   Well, I would like to enter into evidence a different perspective. I would like to submit Exhibit A: *Matthew 6:33...*

> *...and he will give you all you need from day to day if you live*
> *for him and make the Kingdom of God your primary concern."*

Well now you see, if you are spending time with him each day, you are ultimately getting what you need for the day, which makes you a priority! Ok, hopefully you will see this my way. Just in case, let's break this down a little more to its most simple form of understanding. One version of scripture (ERV) does just that. It plainly says,

> *"What you should want most is God's kingdom and doing what*
> *he wants you to do. Then he will give you all these other things*
> *you need."*

Now, I just don't know that it can get much clearer than that! If you seek Him FIRST, everything you need and want...he will give it to you! So see, by focusing on him, you are really focusing on you. Then he gives back to you for focusing on him. Is it really that simple? Is He just going to give me everything that I ask for? First off, let me put to death something that is often heard in conversations today. It's the misconception of **Name it and Claim it**. We have come to believe that if we want something, all we have to do is name it, quote scripture and God is supposed to deliver it to us. Sitting back waiting on God to fulfill our every desire, need, and want on a whelm is absolutely out of the question. He is not a slot machine or magic genie. If we have a relationship with Christ, it is a *partnership* and we each have a role to

God doesn't
need your
Plan of Action.
He is looking
for your Faith
in Action!

play! I believe it says to seek...FIRST, then...we will receive. Many of us are asking God to give us the strength to make it through the day, tame our tongues on the job, help us with the kids, help with the husbands and help us to juggle all the duties for the day. We want to receive strength and power, without seeking HIS presence. We conveniently want to receive, but do not want to be inconvenienced or made to feel uncomfortable if someone holds us accountable. Think about how we feel when our children always want "stuff" that we sacrifice for and give to them, but sulk and become annoyed when we ask them to wash their plate or clean their room. The things that should be eagerly done out of pure gratitude appear to be an intrusion on their day.

Tell the truth, every now and then don't we often respond to our Heavenly Father the way that our children respond to us? Okay, don't raise your hand. I don't need to know, but you do! Unless we recognize it, call it what it is and be willing to change it, our Heavenly Father eventually has to address it, just as we do with our own children. I think you get my point! Let's move on.

So you're searching for the key to your car. You are diligently searching and in pursuit of them. Without that one little piece of metal, weighing less than a few ounces, you can't get to your next destination. Your day will not reach its full level of productivity without that key. Well, in this busy life Christ is the key, literally. Christ must become the priority that we are seeking, first, to give us what we need. This is what will open the door for Him to propel us through the day and on to our various destinations! He must become that single, most important piece AND peace that we seek first thing in the morning, so that our day is fulfilled with all the mercies that we are believing and expecting to receive. This, my dear, is how you are placing yourself at the top of the priority list. You are getting exactly what you need in order to have the strength and stamina to make it through the day.

Ministries often teach and seek out the illustration of the woman in Proverbs 31. This biblical icon, somewhat compared to our modern-day Olivia Pope, always has it under control. Although she had servants, she still woke up before dawn to start her day. Come on now, tell the true, how many of you would stay in bed just a little longer or indulge in that bubble bath more often if you had servants and maids coming in to take care of your household? Wait a minute. Don't raise your hands so fast or you'll drop the book! Seriously, she could have stayed in bed, slept late and waited for her breakfast to be brought to her. Oh no, not this woman! She understood her life's priority. She clearly understood the hierarchy that reigned in her household that produced a JOY that was reflected onto those around her.

Some of our mothers, along with society has guilted us into believing that we must take care of everyone else and if there is time left over, we can spoil ourselves and give Jesus some of our leftover time in the process. Now, don't stone me, just hear me out. If YOU and HIM can't get together, you won't ever be able to get it together with others. Understood that God must be priority in your life, but you are priority in your home.

We are now seeing hundreds of thousands of women...single, married, divorced, and widowed who are unhappy, unfulfilled and stunted in their spiritual growth. We are here, there and everywhere, but really not going anywhere at all...just moving! We are not productive, we are not accomplishing much, better yet, we've not even sought after the dreams, goals or plans that God has set for our lives. In fact, many of us have never partitioned God to find out what our purpose is in life. Why? Because we have become just like those beautiful rocking chairs that we find on the porch of one of my favorite breakfast spots, Cracker Barrel. As pretty as they are, as fast as they can rock, it's really all for naught. They are not going anywhere! That's really the sum total of many of our lives. We are exerting a whole lot of energy moving, going and doing all the "stuff" that we think we are supposed to do, but really going nowhere.

So what do I do to make myself a priority without feeling guilty? The first order of business is for us to commit to intentionally placing and keeping our lives in this order: God (pouring into you through His word), spouse, children and job, whether you work inside or outside of the home. The scriptures are quite clear on this stance and we must be diligent in acting it out. If we learn to start the day seeking God, we will find that our day will be much more productive, peaceful and impactful. We will get more accomplished as our thoughts are directed on what we should do first, or what to do at all. We will find out that we have saved time and exerted less energy in our daily movements and chores. Start your day with 10 minutes of uninterrupted alone time with God. As your relationship grows, you will find that your longing to be with the lover of your soul will increase. Soon you will see that you can't start your day any other way!

Being a wife and mother takes a lot of physical and emotional stamina. If you continue to make home and not yourself priority, eventually there will be a breakdown. Keep saying to yourself that you are the #1 Priority in your home. You are a vital part to the family being a well run machine! So by ensuring that you are physically and mentally healthy, not only will you meet the daily demands with ease, you will have time and stamina to meet the needs of your husband. Sounds like a good time to talk about these fellows whom we love so dearly!

Closing Thoughts- Remember that Home *is* high on the priority list and God is priority in your life. In your home, **you are the #1 Priority.** If you don't take care of yourself, you can't take care of your home. Incorporating these key focuses will help you keep the main thing the main thing:

1. Commit to spending some morning time with your creator and lover of your soul. Start with 10 minutes and allow it to gradually increase.
2. Incorporate some type of exercise into your day. (i.e. walking, yoga, at home exercise video, etc.) This helps your physical, emotional, mental and sexual stamina.
3. Teach your family to respect moments that you need to refuel and replenish. (i.e. 1 hour of interrupted time to relax in the bathtub, a spa day with the girls, etc.)

And remember, ***God doesn't need your Plan of Action, he needs your Faith in Action! Shake it Girl, Shake it! The Breaking has begun!***

*Reflections*_____

_____

_____

_____

_____

_____

Prayer for a Tender and Submissive Heart

Lord, teach me your ways. Forgive me for living a double standard. I pray that Godly individuals penetrate my circle. I pray that they love me enough to hold me accountable with my sometimes manipulative and often bitter disposition. I submit to you Lord and to my husband. Teach me, Oh God for you are my peace and my redeemer.

In your Holy name,
Amen

CHAPTER 4
DON'T PUT NO MAN, NOT EVEN YOUR HUSBAND, BEFORE YOUR KIDS!

Well, even the eyebrows of my mother rose, when I told her the title of this chapter. We have all been influenced by what our mothers, grands and great grands before us have had to endure; the good and the not so pleasant. Through the research of this book, I have listened to the heart wrenching stories of how good, hard working fathers, who took care of their families, got caught up in behaviors and ways of life that were passed down to them by their fathers, grands and great grands who were taught behaviors during enslavement that have not been let go. Behaviors like: it's okay to have a female on the side, as long as it doesn't affect the home front. Now, **that** is like really, some craziness handed down to many males from their fathers. During the slavery era, it was customary on Friday night for the slave owner to take the men away from their wives and to move them to other plantations to mate with females in order to produce more slaves. It was against their will and their strong protective nature, but over a period of time, became a forced way of life. I mean, what do you do? They couldn't exactly tell the slave owner that they weren't going. That's a true beaten waiting to happen, or better yet, a grave with your name on it!

> God considers our feelings, but is not solely moved by them.

From that mindset, it has been adopted that the wife's job is to stay at home with the kid's, while the husband breaks away for the weekend after a long week of work. Really?? Who does that? Many men still do...that's who! Sad but true, many old habits are hard to break and some take years to do so. Many women have lived their lives, suffering in this type of abuse for the sake of the kids and because of what momma said. Mothers encouraged their daughters to stay in the marriage at all costs. Some have been conditioned that even if your husband is unfaithful, he will always come back home. Take care of your children, let him be and keep a stash on the side (which we will talk about in a later chapter)! So, did this decision to stay in such a relationship help or hurt their offspring who were taking notice, better yet, being taught? Let's examine the lie of not putting a man before your kids a little closer.

When we refer, and relate to scripture, **God considers our feelings, but is not always moved by them.** He is more so moved by our obedience. And through obedience, blessings will follow. He expects us to fully hand over our emotions to Him. He knows them already, but looks for us to be honest and truthful with ourselves, so that in our transparency, he can heal, guide and direct. Therefore, what God has joined together, let man not separate.

Our first passage stop in this chapter will be a familiar statement that is found in Mark 10: 7-9 says this...

> For this reason, a man will leave his father and mother and
> be joined to his wife, and the two shall become one flesh. So
> then they are no longer two, but one flesh. Therefore, what
> God has joined together, let not man separate.

Far too long, we have not really taken this statement to heart and really applied it to our marriages. Think of it like this. It is close to impossible to remove every piece of evidence of gum fiber that is stuck to carpet. Why, you ask? Because that gum and carpet have

36

now become one. To remove the gum will mean that you would have to perform surgery and cut the entire area that has been woven into the carpet. The gum is now a part of every carpet fiber that it has attached itself to, making it "one" with the carpet.

Now if, in fact, you are now viewed as one and operating as one, interwoven into the fibers of the other, bone of his bone and flesh of his flesh, it should be next to *impossible* for you to act solely without it affecting your spouse. To be quite honest, it is impossible for you to be blessed in your marriage when you are **not** putting your husband before your kids. I know this is not going to be very popular with this new age group of believers. Time has changed, but God's word hasn't. Let's dive a little deeper.

Right after your sunrise love-fest with your Heavenly Father that we talked about in Chapter 3 and just after you have established yourself as the #1 Priority in the household and even before the kids, is the husband. Did I just feel your eyes roll? Wait a minute.....stop grinding those teeth! This is serious business. Unfortunately, this hierarchy issue is also a major deal for many a wife.

There is a word that has been placed on the "naughty word" list. It's a no-no and we are just not having it. Society has duped the world of women to believe that this ten-letter word is the end of our lives as we would know it. I am sure you know it or at least heard it, because many women have taken a solemn vow not to utter it and certainly, not commit to it. So let me spell it out for you....S..U..B..M..I..S..S..I..O..N. Whew...that wasn't so bad, was it? So, let's say it together...SUBMISSION. One more time just to get it in our head first, before I try to convince you to move it to your heart! Submission. Way to go girl!!! Now, let the shaking begin.

Here, right now, today, what we first must understand is that this word is not a gender-based word! Men, women, children, pets, everyone and everything that has breath submits to something or someone. Submission is for everyone; Believers and non-believers alike. Everyone must submit to someone; a boss, a policeman, a hostess at a restaurant. Oh no, not us, though. We, good ole' church folks, good ole' Christians don't feel the need to submit in most situations. We are even now teaching our children that they too, do not have to submit to authority. We will submit to the pastor at the church house, but how about learning to first submit to the pastors at our house!

I know I am treading into deep waters, but let's learn something here. Take Exhibit A, Ephesians 5:21 says:

...we are to submit ourselves to one another out of reverence
for Christ.

It did not just say wives submit, it says "WE". That means everyone who is a member of the family that Apostle Paul is talking about. Look at 1 Corinthians 11:3. It comes from another perspective so that we don't forget:

Now I want you to realize that the head of every man is
Christ, and the head of the woman is man, and the head of
Christ is God.

Subsequently, we hear this submission word directed mostly to my sisters, but know that men have a responsibility to submit to you, as well. Hopefully, that makes you feel a little better and makes it a little more palatable so that we can move on a little further with your ears and hearts open to receive and then ultimately act.

There is also another passage that I would like to share with you. Can you first just say... "Lord I need this because this is key"? Ok, keep that in mind as you read this passage found in Philippians 2:5.

It reads like this...

"Your attitude should be the same as that of Christ Jesus."
Ok, this can be a long road or a short one, it's your choice. Either way, we have started this awesome journey, so let's do it!

We, sisters, must adjust our negative, hard, bitter and harsh attitudes. In the event we don't realize that we need an adjustment, this is where we must have and allow our Christian sisters to help call us into accountability. You just read it! He didn't ask or suggest, it's a command that we have an attitude of Christ. Hear what I am saying! This is a major blessing blocker! We would see more victory in our lives if we would monitor and adjust our attitudes. Don't you dare pretend that you don't know what I'm talking about! We have ALL been there a time or two. Oh, we may comply with what our husbands or future spouse have suggested, asked or requested, but the attitude that we bring with it cancels out the fact that we complied. If we focus on doing what's right, in the right way, God **promises** to deal with what's left. Even if what's left are broken hearts, damaged feelings, emotional pain and deferred hopes and dreams. Remember this...**God Always Has You in Mind!**

Keep in mind, again, God holds you responsible for how you treat others, not how they treat you! I can already hear you..."Come on! You just don't understand." You are correct, my dear; in some cases I don't and in some I do. But one thing for sure that I do understand is... God knows all the cases, yep, every single one of them. Even that one that's deep in the corner of your heart that no one knows about. And he still expects for you to trust him. He says cast your cares on Him, not your responsibility. Once again, you have a responsibility to be an example. You have a responsibility to manage your home and your environment in a way that will make God and your spouse look good. Yes, him too! We have a responsibility to honor and respect our husbands, if married and our future husbands, if in a committed relationship that is moving towards marriage. We have a responsibility that can model and shape the rest of our lives. And as long as we try to fix it through our manipulative dispositions, behaviors and attitudes, God will not help us. Manipulative, "Are you serious? I am not manipulative", you say. Oh, but I differ. It's in us. From the beginning of time, Eve convinced Adam through her manipulation to abdicate the directives that God clearly gave to him. And we are still doing it today. Well grant it, we have become a little more sophisticated since Eve's day. Your way may be different than another, based on what has worked for you, when you got your way or what you wanted. Let me be the bearer of bad news for a second. My sister, it doesn't matter which way it is delivered, it's all manipulation. Whether you cry when you don't get your way, you dish out the silent treatment, or how about this one...withholding sex until we get what we want; Ding, Ding...MANIPULATION. I know of one young lady whose husband is up for work at 4:00 a.m. Her tactic is to keep him awake all night until he just gives in! Come on ladies, we cannot do this! Not only are we creating resentment in our relationships, but we are so far away from God's intent, his character and his will. If we have the faith that God will take care of us, let's trust him on that alone. But don't forget that our responsibility is to walk in obedience to God and to our husbands. I don't remember who said this, but partial obedience is full time disobedience.

Hopefully, you are a little more comfortable with the idea of spending time with God so that you have what you need to be the #1 Priority in your home and with the word submission. Because in your life, right after God, he expects your husband to be there. If

your husband is the leader in your home, (and he should be),
Hebrews 13: 17 is what we must make some reference to...

> *Obey those who rule over you, and be submissive, for they*
> *watch out for your souls, as those who must give an account.*
> *Let them do so with joy and not with grief, for that would be*
> *unprofitable for you.*

Understand that I, in no way, am saying that being submissive
means that a wife has no input. An example of a wife's input is
demonstrated in Genesis 21:11 when God tells Abraham to listen
and do whatever Sarah tells him to do about a matter that was
stressing the brother out.   And because he listened, both seeds
were blessed, even though Sarah's attempt of control seemed more
logical than trusting God in the first place. This directive happened
because of both persons being led by the voice of
God. The moment your husband asked or forces you
to do something that doesn't line up with the word
of God, he just handed his headship over to Christ
and your submission then is to God. Now, I'm
talking about things that are clearly contradicting to
God's word...stealing, cheating, murder, upholding
what you both know is disobedient and sinful acts.

Trust
always
incites
obedience.

Don't you dare start justifying decisions that we make that have
absolutely nothing to do with God, but everything to do with us
disagreeing with the leader of your household and the very one who
is charged with guarding and watching out for your soul! You know
what I'm talking about! Hubby says don't charge anything else on
that card, you do it anyway and hide the bag in the trunk of the car
until you can sneak it into the house just at the time he goes to
work. I know how it works! Believe it or not, I've pulled that once or

twice. That may be a small issue, but trust me, if we do not recognize and address these small infestations, we can find ourselves in patterns that eventually will be spiraling out of control.

Once these issues take on new life, we begin to take on an attitude of defiance. As the leader and watcher of your soul, God holds him accountable for you and the path that he leads the family on. Your attitude of defiance now makes it difficult for your leader to lead. Often our past hurts and fears, gives us false credence to override our leader's voice until they become passive fixtures in the museums that we call home. They are there physically, but with no voice, no respect and no support. So, let's shake off the fear to submit and allow that man to take his rightful place! Seek Godly counsel on when and how to provide that input. We are so adamant about giving our input, that we want God's way to become our way. NOT...God doesn't need our help in this matter, even if our spouse is wrong! It is a humbling and often a painful experience to learn to respectfully be quiet and trust that God will impress upon our leader's heart the will and the way that he should go. In submission, lies your true strength as you trust in God to allow your 'Abraham' to lead the way. Remember, trust always incites obedience.

One last thought...Submission is easy when it's a reciprocation of a husband's leadership. Ok, Ok... I hear you. You say that in your reflection you admit that you have been that overriding, nagging voice that has lead your husband to lead passively, not lead at all or just comply to your demands. Well, it's up to you now, to give him the reigns back! You shake free so that you can free others.

Financial investments are predictable in that the more you deposit consistently and often, the more bountiful your benefits will be when it comes time for you to reap and withdraw. Marriages are quite similar. Six months shy of 50 years of marriage to my father before his passing, my mother reminds my brothers and their wives, that marriage is an investment. It is an investment that brings along high and low risks, but your commitment to stay the course will allow you to be a beneficiary of the blessings that come from what a loving leader and a respectful completer can become. Those sometimes subtle and yet impactful deposits into the marriage investment account could be the gentle stroke of your leader's ego or perhaps that willingness to hold off on that conversation until a more conducive time when he's not coming home from a frustrating day at work. You must be willing to take the time to learn your leader enough to know what that investment must to be to yield the best return. And since he was created by the heavenly father that would be a great starting point. As you will come to read in my future book, small things really mean a lot and can make a difference in your relationships. If acted upon, by creating the environment for our Kings to thrive, you will receive a return on your investment that is multiplied exponentially! I am so thankful that in God's economy, God multiplies and not just adds! Aren't you glad about that, too?

One of the benefits that you will find in walking in obedience of God's divine order of headship, is relational fulfillment with a spouse that you have built a permanent unshakeable foundation. Only when you have neglected to disciple your children to become responsible, independent thinkers, will they feel the need to stay beneath your wings. Children do leave, eventually and will have their own friends, their own lives, their own spouses and children. So, choosing to make your spouse your primary investment, respecting him as your lordship and making sure that he is in his rightful place, before your children, is a very wise investment. You are not merely building a relationship, you are setting the stage to reap blessings that you will be able to model and leave a roadmap for your children, grandchildren and generations to come to follow; All by going against the norm and doing it God's way!

Closing Thoughts- Consider doing some real honest soul searching and heart checking. Get yourself under subjection and start walking in your role as a respectful completer. Stop praying for him so much and pray for yourself! Pray that God will reveal the areas of growth for you. Pray that you can be the supporter and the completer that God has called you to be for your husband. Ask God to forgive you for contributing to the damage that you have caused to your relationship and show you how to begin to repair the wounds that you have created through your words and your often-manipulative actions. You are one! What hurts him, will have a hurtful effect upon you. Once he takes the reins back, especially for the first time, it will be a struggle; for you and for him. But God will honor your submission and blessings will begin to flow through you and on to your children, all because you were willing to shake off the lie of putting your children before your husband! Keep shaking girl. You are on your way to breaking free!

*Reflections*_____

_____

_____

_____

_____

_____

Prayer for Honor

Your word says to give honor where honor is due. I repent, Father God, for not doing a good job of that in my house. I have unknowingly and sometimes knowingly dishonored my spouse, with my words and my actions. I have often not empowered, encouraged or supported. Convict me at the very moment that my speech doesn't line up with your heart for my mate. Help me to communicate and create the boundaries that you have laid out for a Godly family. I praise you in advance for victory in being the Godly wife and mother that you have called me to be.

In your matchless name,
Amen

CHAPTER 5
ALWAYS KEEP A SECRET STASH

I wish I could say, as Gomer Pyle would say, "Surprise, Surprise, Surprise". But honestly, this was no surprise at all. Keep in mind, that we are exposing lies. And who do we know to be the master deceiver of these lies? Correct, Satan! We have gotten comfortable with mixing a spoonful of lies with the barrel of truth. We have forgotten that it only takes that one little spoonful to wipe us out. You say you don't know if you believe me... Well, you just go ahead and try that same tactic with a nice tall glass of ice cold lemonade and a spoon full of poison. What will you have? Well, my friends, you will have a dead body on your hands. It may take a little longer before it infects the whole-body system, but if you keep believing that a glass of 99% lemonade will cancel out the 1% of poison, you have written a prescription for a slow death.

Obviously, we are not referring to physical death. But spiritual death here on earth can be just as bad, if not worse. Death of the relationship with Him, death of truth, death of intimacy, no matter which area, this flat-lined diagnosis does not have to be the final announcement.

Many of us have prescribed to this notion or lie for most, if not all our lives. Really, you have got to be kidding me! What in the world could be wrong with me keeping a "secret" stash? That's what my momma said and I don't see anything wrong with it. Sister, I hear the voices in your head, the clearing of your throats, the crackling of your voices and I even see the neck and rolling of the eyes! But just hear

There is no place for secrets in a relationship!

me out first. There is absolutely nothing wrong with having a stash.
In fact, you should always have a stash or a little something set aside
for emergencies, that special surprise gift or for that birthday trip
that you want to surprise him with. The concern is not the stash, my
dear diva sister …the 1% of poison is the "secret". Secrets have no
place in a marriage…no place, zero place, no hay lugar *(that's no
place in Spanish)*.. especially not with finances. Let's hurry and take
a plunge into this before you close the book on me.

A paraphrased definition of secret is something that is not
known or seen or not meant to be known or seen by others. Ok, I
see you are not convinced with that definition from the dictionary.
Perhaps we read it too fast, so let's approach it from a different
light. Anytime we have an unhealthy view about anything, there is a
greater possibility of misuse or mishandling. Now I am not saying
that saving or having a stash is an unhealthy exercise, but what is
your motive for <u>keeping</u> the stash a secret? If we understand that
ultimately, everything we have belongs to God, and it is only by His
provisions that we have anything, there is no need to hide it. "I
know that God knows where it is, but my husband doesn't!" I hear
you loud and clear! Think back to chapter one…*There is nothing
hidden that will not be made evident*. Do you think for one minute
that God cannot expose a bank account, money hidden under the
spare tire or in a shoe box in the back of the kitchen pantry? First,
it's all His…Secondly, it's all His and Thirdly, it's all His! **I hope you
are hearing me.**

I get it, my sister. I have heard and even witnessed a mother
scrapping up money just to make sure her kids had what they
needed because the father spent the money doing God only knows
what, with God only knows who! So, if that is your situation, you

have the right to have a stash, but you still don't have the right for it to be a secret. Firstly, if that is your situation, the male in your home is not operating under the rule or authority of God. But that still doesn't justify disrespect of headship and deceptive maneuvers. Whoa, wait a minute...I felt those daggers! Give me a moment and let me get them out of my back. Ok, ok, so now that I know how you feel about this touchy subject, I obviously need some powerful backup. So, let's look at Hebrews 13:5:

> *"Keep your lives free from the love of money and be content with what you have, because God has said, "Never will I leave you; never will I forsake you."*

So, if we trust that God will never leave us or forsake us, why do we have to hide anything? Why would we need to maintain a secret? Here is why the enemy loves secrets. Secrets are subtle ways to create deception. Deception produces an opportunity for the enemy to cast thoughts of imagination and create doubt and distrust. Before you know it, questions start to arise like, "Why are you saving money?" "So what else are you doing that I don't know about?", just to state a few. And if they don't come out and say it to you, most will think it or utter it to a close friend in the gym locker room. Now that seed of distrust has been planted and waits for other opportunities to happen that add water to that growing seed. Given some time and more imaginary thoughts, that seed is now a full-grown tree with stubborn roots that are hard to move otherwise.

How do we resolve this? Despite what your mother taught you, communicate openly about your finances. Our mothers and our grandmothers had to do what was necessary for them at *that* time. Ladies, we don't have to continue that tradition. Our times are very different. I don't know about you, but just give it to me straight. I don't want to have to figure it out or read between the lines. Well, if you are like me, then you will get what Paul said in 1 Timothy 4:7:

"Have nothing to do with godless myths and old wives' tales; rather train yourself to be godly."

Really? I mean come on now...that's as clear as the ocean water in Belize! In many areas, we have unintentionally been taught wrong teachings and told these wives tales that worked during that era. But it's now time for us to renew our minds from this kind of thinking and allow God's simplistic word to set us free.

This reminds me of a story that has been shared about a newlywed couple who decided to cook Sunday dinner together for the bride's family. As the eager new husband watched his new bride prepare a ham, she removed the outer wrap, cut off the end of the ham, and then threw the end of the ham into the trash. "Honey, why did you through that part of the ham away?" asked the husband. "It's the way my mother taught me how to cook the ham," the young bride replied. "Why did your mother do that?" asked the husband. "Well, I don't know." "Could you ask her?" As the wife agreed, she went to her mother and asked. "Mother, when you cook a ham, why do you cut off the end and throw it away?" "Well, my dear, it's the way your grandmother taught me to do it. You'll need to ask her," said the mother. So the bride went to her grandmother with the same question. "Sweet child," the grandmother laughed, "I cut off the end of the ham because the ham was always too big to fit into the pot!"

Many times we develop our way of life in much of the same way. We mimic what we have heard or seen and repeat it question. We don't challenge or question these teachings because we have been "taught" by someone whom we love and trust. They are, in most cases, loving, good, kind and sincere people.

What we fail to remember is that those people have, in the same way, been taught by decent people that they trusted and loved, so beliefs and advice continue unchallenged generation after generation. If the new bride had taken the stance of "Honey, this is the way my mother did it and if it's good for her, it's good for me, she would have never learned the truth about the ham.

So now let's apply this to us now. We often know that there are pieces of advice and information being shared that is obviously not in God's word. However, we trust our mothers so we continue on living that principle. Stop cutting off the end of the ham and question, compare and research why these lies still exist.

Regarding this principle of keeping a stash, share your concerns with your spouse and present the fact that although you have a "stash", be open and honest about your intent and purpose for these funds.

If it's a situation where money is being abused by your spouse, still make it your business to let them know that you have it only for those times when unwise choices have been made. Together, if possible, set the boundaries on how and when this money will be utilized. Setting boundaries has the potential to demonstrate that it is better to have a little with the fear of the Lord than have a lot of wealth with turmoil in your household with your spouse. Single women, have this conversation early on. Share the level of comfort that you have about seeing your mother having to have a secret stash in order to keep things afloat in the household. Create those boundaries early; with God's guidance it will be clear that the enemy has no place for secrets and deception in your family!

Closing Thoughts- The idea of having a stash, if communicated with a healthy relationship mindset about money, is a wise situation. However, having a **secret** stash is not healthy or wise. If you are married, you are one flesh, so everything you do affects the one you are joined with. If you are single, having a stash is smart. Emergencies will always arise. Being disciplined enough to have money set aside shows that you are responsible with the funds that God has allowed you to manage. So, don't keep that stash a secret when Boaz finds you. Don't give Satan any room in your relationship to plant a garden of doubt or seeds of distrust!

*Reflections*_____

_____

_____

_____

_____

_____

Prayer for Honesty

Father, search my heart and reveal YOUR truth to me. Help me to be fearless when being open and honest with you and those who love me. Forgive me for what I have hidden in the past and forgive me for not fully trusting you. Give me an understanding heart and a teachable spirit, so that I may take heart the spiritual lessons that You have me to learn so that I can be used by you, Thank you.

In Jesus' name.
Amen

CHAPTER 6
I'M COMING OUT!

One of the most compelling, yet motivational stories I have heard on the speaking circuit goes a little like this:

One day, a little boy visited the circus with his dad. Although he was having a great time, he was there to see his favorite animal. At the turn of each corner, he patiently waited for the moment. Underneath the big top, there it was! There was the animal that he has waited so patiently to see...the elephants! This enormous creature with big flapping ears. His trunk tickled the little boy's hand as he fed him one peanut at a time. The little boy was so excited as he examined every inch of the elephant. He then noticed something. The lad noticed that this huge creature was being held by a small rope, not a heavy chain or a cage, but a thin rope. Even the young child knew that the elephant could break free from the ropes if it wanted to. "Excuse me," the lad said to the elephant trainer who was nearby. "Why does this huge elephant, have such a small rope? Aren't you afraid that they will break free?" The trainer bent down to one knee to speak to the lad. "Well son, when the elephants are very young, just about your height, we use a rope about that size to tie them down. At that age, it's enough to hold them. But as they grow and become older, they are so used to being tied up that they believe that they cannot break free. They believe the rope can still hold them, so they never try to break free from their situation."

Come on now...I am going somewhere, but I hope you are down the street waving at me! Many of us are just like the elephants at the circus. At any point, we could break free from the lies, the bondage and the mindsets that we have been so conditioned to believe. But what momma said or what grandmother told us, becomes that tiny rope that keeps us stuck in bondage. So, we continue to go around and around that same circle. We are maneuvering through life hanging on to outdated beliefs that have no biblical doctrine or reasoning. Continuing to hold on to those lies that hinder our relationships with those around and most importantly, with the Master, Our Heavenly Father.

A very familiar passage in scripture is John 8:32. I am quite sure you have heard in and at some point, maybe even quoted it. See if this sounds familiar...

> "...And you will know the truth, and the truth will set you free."

The truth, my sisters, is that it is time for us to BREAK FREE. We have been stuck in our situations far too long. Some of us have been there so long, that we have now decorated the walls and made it home! I am here to help you understand that the location of your life has already been placed in heavenly place. It is without question that if we want to walk in victory, we must change our mindsets from what momma said to what God says!

What God says is more important than what Momma said!

Our mothers and grandmothers did the best they could with the knowledge, skills and information that they had. But as the old saying goes, "When you know better, do better." Ladies, it's time for us to do better! God has called us to be women of character, role models for our daughters and mentors for other young women. He loves us so much that he wants nothing more than to have a daily intimate relationship with us. He promises that this relationship with Him will not only change the fibers of our lives, but the very fabric of our family's lives. *Knowing* the truth is one thing, but now <u>accepting</u> it is what makes the difference. We should do some self-reflecting, I mean true, honest self-reflecting so that we can recognize where we have stood on Momma's words instead of our Heavenly Father's words. Trust me! I know that it's not going to be easy. In fact you will feel like it is just down-right impossible. This change has to be intentional. We have to make the decision to include God in the plan to walk in this journey. Let's be clear. This intentional decision to include God in every component of your lives will not be popular with your Facebook friends. It may result in you having to eat lunch alone in the workplace. You may have to even miss a few family functions or friendly outings. Now don't get me wrong, I absolutely love a social event, a good jazz lounge or a local music festival. The concern becomes when you surround yourself with individuals who do not have the same mindset. Being a representative for Christ is not a list of do's and do not's. But it is a decision to make what God said more important than what your momma said and standing firm on that.

I was told by a young lady that her mother told her that it was ok to "dip". Can you believe that? Maybe you are like me and had no clue what she was saying. Well, this is what that means. It's okay to sleep around as long as you don't get attached to them, while you use protection, of course. Let's all say it on the count of 3- 1...2...3...CRAZY!!!! That is so crazy on so many different levels that we will have to talk about it in a book to come or one of our girl talk roundtable sessions. These are the types of lies that we have to rid ourselves from less we continue on this path of heart hurt and mental turmoil. Are we perfect? Absolutely not. But we are chosen and crowned as royalty. Therefore, there are just certain things that we don't do if we value ourselves and believe our creator.

Jeremiah 29:11 teaches us that God has a plan for each of us. It's a plan to prosper us and not harm us. It's a plan that will give us hope and a future. That means we don't have to live these reckless lives that continue to cause us to wander aimless through life. He has a plan for us if we are willing to follow it. Keep in mind that God never gives us a plan without the power and resources to fulfill it. One resource is your sister or sisters who have walked through this tool-kit journey with you. Lean on each other. Hold each other accountable and continue to walk in the new truth that has set you free!

I may be dating myself here, but Diana Ross, a famous artist who started her career with the Motown group, Supremes, created a song that I believe can be the theme song for this chapter. It's entitled, you guessed it...I'm Coming. Just listen to some of the lyrics...

I'm coming out
I want the world to know
Got to let it show
I'm coming out
There's a new me coming out
And I just had to live
And I want to give
I'm completely positive
I am gonna do it
Oh, I'll make it through it

The time has come for me to break out of this shell
I just have to shout that I am coming out!
I've got to show the world, all that I want to be
And all my abilities, There's so much more to me
There's no need to fear, And I just feel glad
Every time I hear, I'm Coming Out!

Do you get my point? We have to be willing to get off the gossip lines. Turn off the internet, log off of FaceBook, Snap Chat and Twitter sometimes and spend time focusing on what will ultimately make a positive difference in our lives and the lives of our family.

Closing Thoughts- We live in a world where everything is public and going viral. I pray that the notion to Break Free from these lies that we have discussed will take root and move through our lives like a wild fire. It's difficult for us to help free the next generation if we ourselves are still bound by the same perpetual choices.

In conversations, I hear elderly women speak in dismay about today's generation of young woman. Sometimes I weigh in offering hopefully a positive solution or outlook. Most of the time I just listen in silence. How many countless lives have been ruined by these lies that our mothers taught us? We have wives holding fast to what momma did or did not do. Instead of communicating to find out what will make your relationship one that will be a model for others to follow. I am seeing young ladies who have seen a cycle of abuse and now unconsciously gravitate from one unhealthy abusive relationship to another. I am often disappointed at the fact that these "mothers" continue to offer ungodly advice and expect a Godly outcome. It's past the time to break free and come out!

A good friend and business partner would often open a business meeting by asking, "If you are lost in the wilderness, do you run faster or stop and get your bearings?" Almost resembling a chorus, the group would answer, "Stop running". If it's that simple to understand, why then are we running through life? Not only are we running through it, but we are lost, falling down, losing time, getting hurt and bruised, while getting farther and farther away from the path that He has already laid for us. Stop and get your bearings! Get on a routine of studying, mediation and reflection. By doing so, He will lead us to the right path and walk us into the life that He has waiting for you!

*Reflections*_____

_____

_____

_____

_____

_____

Prayer for Spiritual Growth

Heavenly Father, how I thank you and praise you for you are a Good Father. You long for us to connect with you and depend on you. This is my heart's desire. I pray, Lord, that I can become more like you so that my life will bear much fruit.

Fill my heart with your compassion and kindness so that I may truly love. Thank you in advance, for making me more like you. Help me to manage my time better, so that I can devote my heart and my time to reflect on what you have done, what you are doing and what you are going to do in my life, so that you will be magnified more in my life. I submit to you, Father and I willfully ask that you root out any bad attitudes, foolish thoughts and conversations, or wrong motives that may start to formulate in my heart or mind, that will hinder my growth to be more like you. I commit myself victorious! Help me continue to be a glory and not a shame as I profess Thy name.

In your Holy name I pray,
Amen

7 CHAPTER
TOOLS TO BREAK FREE

Breaking the chains from bondages in our lives is not an easy feat. They are patterns that have been set and actions that we have lived out for years. So, re-training our thoughts and taking every thought captive is a not a daily process, but a moment by moment process.

These scripture cards are simply tools that you can use to fill your environment and atmosphere with the word of God that speaks specifically to the area of struggle in your life. Put them on your bathroom mirror, so that you can speak these words to yourself first thing in the morning. Place them in your car so that you are reminded "whose" you are and what your heavenly daddy says about you. Display them in your cubical at work so that you are reminded in your interaction with others that you have received the mercy that He freely gives and is strengthening you to help other sisters walk through this process of breaking free from these chains that keep us from living a fulfilled and rewarding life.

So, make as many copies as you would like. Then commit to memorizing just one or two a week. As you are memorizing them, begin to speak these words into your life and into the lives of the sisters who are holding you accountable. Remove yourself from anyone and anything that is contradicting what the word of God is saying. Not over night, but soon, you will see and feel the strength that you need to... *Break Free from the Lies that Our Mothers Taught Us...*one lie at a time!

Isaiah 43:25

I, even I, am he who blots out your transgressions, for my own sake, and remembers your sins no more.

1 Corinthians 14:40

But everything should be done in a fitting and orderly way.

Micah 7: 18

Who is a God like you, who pardons sin and forgives the transgression of the remnant of his inheritance? You do not stay angry forever but delight to show mercy. You will again have compassion on us; you will tread our sins underfoot and hurl all our iniquities into the depths of the sea.

2 Corinthians 12:9-10

But he said to me, "my grace is sufficient for you, for my power is made perfect in your weakness."

Psalms 72:12

For he will deliver the needy who cry out, the afflicted who have no one to help.

Psalm 103:6

The Lord gives righteousness and justice to all who are treated unfairly.

Isaiah 38: 17

Surely it was for my benefit that I suffered such anguish. In your love, you kept me from the pit of destruction; you have put all my sins behind your back.

Romans 5:5

...and hope does not put us to shame, because God's love has been poured into our hearts through the Holy Spirit who has been given to us.

Hebrews 13:17

Obey your leaders and submit to their authority. They keep watch over you as men who must give an account. Obey them so that their work will be a joy, not a burden, for that would be of no advantage to you.

1 John 1:9

If we confess our sins, he is faithful and just and will forgive us our sins and purify us from all unrighteousness.

Psalm 103:6

The Lord gives righteousness and justice to all who are treated unfairly.

2 Corinthians 5:17

Therefore, if anyone is in Christ, he is a new creation; the old has gone, the new has come!

Colossians 3:13

Bear with each other and forgive whatever grievances you may have against one another. Forgive as the Lord forgave you.

Proverbs 14:1

The wise woman builds her house, but with her own hands the foolish one tears her down.

Ephesians 5:22 -23

Wives, submit to your husband as to the Lord. For the husband is the head of the wife as Christ is the head of the church, his body, of which he is the Savior.

James 1:12

Blessed is the man who preservers under trial, because when he has stood the test, he will receive the crown of like that God has promised to those who love him.

Ephesians 4: 29

Do not let any unwholesome talk come out of your mouths, but only what is helpful for building others up according to their needs, that it may benefit those who listen.

Proverbs 25:15

Through patience a ruler can be persuaded, and a gentle tongue can break a bone.

Deuteronomy 31:6

Be strong and courageous. Do not fear or be in dread of them, for it is the LORD your God who goes with you. He will not leave you or forsake you.

Titus 3:1-2

Remind the people to be subject to rulers and authorities, to be obedient, to be ready to do whatever good, to slander no one, to be peaceable and considerate, and to show true humility toward all men.

Philippians 4:6-7

Do not be anxious about anything, but in everything by prayer and petition, with thanksgiving, present your requests to God. And the peace of God, which transcends all understanding, will guard your hearts and your minds in Christ Jesus.

Hebrews 12:1

Therefore, since we are surrounded by such a great cloud of witnesses, let us throw off everything that hinders and the sin that so easily entangles, and let us run with perseverance the race marked out for us.

Philippians 4:8

Finally, brothers, whatever is true, whatever is noble, whatever is right, whatever is pure, whatever is lovely, whatever is admirable – if anything is excellent or praiseworthy—think about such things.

Proverbs 15:16

Better a little with the fear of the Lord than great wealth with turmoil.

Hebrews 13:5

Keep your lives free from the love of money and be content with what you have, because God has said, "Never will I leave you; never will I forsake you."

Isaiah 40:31

But those who hope in the LORD will renew strength, They will soar on wings like eagles; they will run and not grow weary, they will walk and not be faint.

_____'s
(Your Name)

Daily Declaration

I declare that I am blessed with God's supernatural wisdom and I have clear direction for my life. I declare that I am blessed with creativity, with courage, with ability, and with abundance.

I declare that I am blessed with a strong will and with self-control and self-discipline. I declare that I am blessed with a great family, with good friends, with good health, and with faith, favor and fulfillment.

I declare that I am blessed with an obedient heart and with a positive outlook on life. I declare that any curse that has ever been spoken over me, any negative evil word that has ever come against me, is broken right now!

I declare that I am blessed in the city, in the country, when I go in and when I come out. I declare that everything that I put my hands to do is going to prosper and succeed.

I Declare that I Am Blessed!

ABOUT THE AUTHOR

Charlotte M. Watson, a seasoned educator, business owner, bible teacher and mediator, blends her passion for the Word of God with an enthusiasm for true sisterhood to create a compelling self-reflective "toolkit". By using a unique combination of light humor and biblical wisdom, *Breaking Free: Living Beyond the Lies that Our Mothers Taught Us*, introduces you to practical life-changing knowledge which will enlighten and strengthen you through the word of God with prayers and scripture.

For Inquiries or Information, write to:
Charlotte M. Watson
P.O. Box 1051
Lancaster, Texas 75146-9998